Chasing the Dragon

Selected Poems

Reyn Kinzey

Deltaville, Virginia

© Copyright 2022 Reyn Kinzey
All Rights Reserved

ISBN: 978-1-945990-49-6

Published by High Tide Publications, Inc.
www.hightidepublications.com

Thank you for purchasing an authorized edition of *Chasing the Dragon.*

High Tide's mission is to find, encourage, promote, and publish the work of authors. We are a small, woman-owned enterprise that is dedicated to the author over 50. When you buy an authorized copy, you help us to bring their work to you.

When you honor copyright law by not reproducing or scanning any part (in any form) without our written permission, you enable us to support authors, publish their work, and bring it to you to enjoy.

We thank you for supporting our authors.

Edited by Cindy L. Freeman cindy@cindylfreeman.com

Book Design and etching by Firebellied Frog Graphic Design

www.firebelliedfrog.com

Please visit the author's website at www.ReynKinzey.com

Dedication

This book is for Rebecca Day,
who believed in these poems
before I did.

Contents

1998 - 1999

Continent of Fire

Everything that rises must converge

It begins here:

The slow ascent
up Humpback Rocks.
Trail muddy with melting snow,
slipping underfoot,
caking on boots.
The new year's sun
gleaming through bare trees.
The trail rising to the rocks,
to the view of endless valley.
Rocks, trees, mountains, light:
The face of eternity.

Or was it here:

Gray rocks
against the green
of Ireland.
Green of rain,
gray of suffering.
Rough, bare heels,
or on the knees.
The slow ascent
up Croagh Patrick.
Flesh pressing against gray rock,
merging with red blood,
sign of salvation.

Or perhaps here:

Rough ladders
nailed into rocks,
straight vertical
viewing Machu Picchu.
Fear the only obstacle.
The path open,
in English,
Spanish,
Quechua,
to men, women.
La hoya no es una droga.

Now, here:

Jazz, jig, or flute,
sounds in the mountain air,
or memories of the past
opening paths,
pushing, pulling us
to the same
or different summits.
In the Shenandoah
in the Andes
on the Continent of Fire.

1998/2001/2004

What I Remember

You showed me Italy.
I showed you Ireland.
Fair trade, I thought.
I tried to show you faith.
I failed.
You showed me beauty.
You won.

I showed you Ballintubber Abbey,
site of loss, suffering,
perseverance, redemption.
Gray rocks against the green of Ireland.
Green of rain,
gray of suffering.
Rough, bare heels--knees, if you're really pious--
the slow ascent up Croagh Patrick,
flesh pressing against gray rock,
merging with red blood,
pink flowers of salvation.
It's an old story, wholly commendable.
But we merely saw, missed the experience.

Italy is impossible to miss,
even in the spring rain.
The Vatican, Saint Peter's Square,
arms outstretched for all.
The Medici Chapel in Florence--
stairs flowing out into space,
ready for the easy ascent.
Michelangelo, smiling, not quite innocently,
waiting around the corner,
inviting us in.

But what I remember
is the market in Rome.
We invaded,
running out of the rain,
yellow slickers soaked,
laughing at the easy victory.
The Visigoths returned.
They mistook us for students
and for Germans
(blonde hair, blue eyes),
yet filled our sandwiches with prosciutto
for half the going price,
inviting us in.

December, 1998

Half-Time on the River

for Becky

At forty, rugby gave way to kayaking.
Cracked fingers no longer healed
without giving way to arthritis.
Concussions came too frequently,
and I'd lost a step
I never really had.

You showed me the river.
It wasn't easy.
The boat didn't want to go straight.
Nothing came naturally
except leaning into the rocks.

But gradually I traded
the adrenaline rush of trys
for the rush of rapids,
the drop, the spray in the face,
the thrill of not being upside down.

After running Choo-Choo,
the rocks' warmth,
lying in the sun
halfway home on the run.
Summer, playing in cool water,
like a whirlpool.
Winter, alone on the river,
watching muskrats
bodysurfing after fish.

Halfway home.
The 40s sliding by.

The frantic dash
to bring the ball back to the forwards,
given over. A younger man's job.
Mine now to balance
the rhythms of water, rock and light.
Halftime on the river,
waiting to play the game to come.

February, 1999

I'm Only Bleeding

for Rene

Part of me is only happy
when I'm bleeding.
From rugby, from mountain biking.
I mean, I'm not a masochist.
I don't like a lot of blood.
Just a scrape or two
to let me know I'm alive.

Like you feel when you follow a run down
with the brakes squealing
'cause you know you're going too fast.
And you see the downward run is followed
by a sixty-degree ascent
on sandy trail
followed by a quick,
hard turn to the right
followed by a steep
downward run
followed by a sixty-degree
ascent on sandy trail
followed by a quick
hard turn to the left.

And it's ninety degrees
and eighty percent humidity under the trees.
Childhood weather of Virginia.
Here near Yorktown
where we turned the world upside down
only two centuries ago,
a century after we turned it upside down
for the Mattaponi,
who used to hunt these trails.

But that was then.
This is now.

My childhood friend
lets me find the path,
take the scrapes.
And the time flies by,
and the trail runs on
through the heat and humidity
through a little sweat and blood.
While the earth and sky bleed for us,
as they have, millennium upon millennium.

Summer, 1999

Gentle Rain of Heaven

"Now, Shakespeare, he's in the alley..."

August, the heat builds in Richmond.
The heat of the presses added to our misery.
But some of us were young.
Lunch break, the basketball backboard called,
and some of us responded.
We played together, sweated together,
and returned to work, more miserable than ever,
but glad, glad to have played.

I said "we."
From June to August I began to notice
I was the only white guy who played.
Glen, the manager,
Bill, the only other white guy,
never played, never joined us.
Both good and decent men:
No statement, just not part of the game.
And me, no statement, either.
A game was there, so I played.

But August the heat builds in Richmond.
Humidity and air close in.
Just before you can't breathe,
the storm.
The storm that cannot be ignored:
lightning pitched beyond belief,
thunder to shake mountains,
commanding respect, if not obedience.

Glen would tell us to shut down the machines.
We would gather around the delivery door.
Bill would open the bays; all of us would sit still,
under the tin roof, safe, dry,
watching the lightning
and the rain driving down.
Watching together, silent, together,
each man content with his own thoughts,
while the merciful rain of heaven rained down,
and our silence was not strained.

Fall, 1999

Sea Lions Barking at the Bay Club

for Juan Rodriquez Cabrillo

Full moon in December,
walking back from Miguel's,
tequila and burritos
like thirty pounds of fish in the stomach.
Halfway back to the hotel,
sea lions barking,
at men on the beach,
sharks in the water.
Who knows why?
A sad, recognizable sound.

Three o'clock, the barking wakes me.
They're on the beach below the hotel.
No laughing matter now, they're unhappy.
I hear you breathing beside me,
I listen to their sound,
And my mind wanders.

To Juan Rodriquez, dying alone,
or surrounded by his men,
Who knows?
He'd waded through the bloodbaths of Mexico,
from Portugal to the New World's shore,
bigger than life, only
to die on the Channel Islands,
looking west for China,
east for the river,
or gold,
or God knows what.
Where did his thoughts turn as the sun set?

Or you, Walt Whitman,

You think you're immune?
On California's shore, facing west,
wondering why we've never found
what we started out for so long ago.
Did you find what you looked for
in poetry or notoriety?

The millennium rushes toward us.
I listen to the sea lions' call,
and I wonder.
Wasn't it always here,
what we've searched for so long,
between the sea lion's yelp
and the receding waves of the sea?

Christmas, anno domini 1999

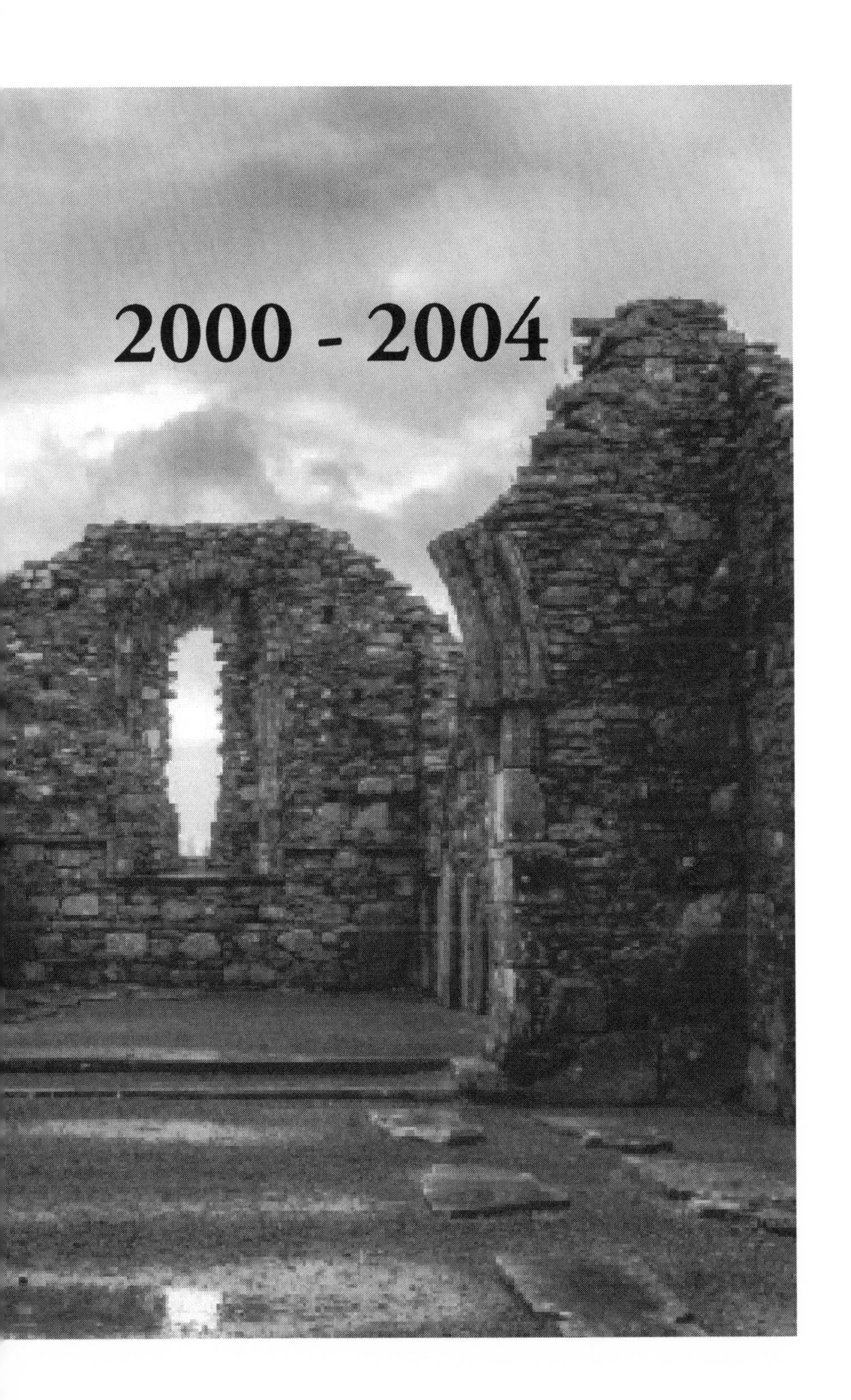
2000 - 2004

Brother to Dragons, 2000

"Bring him here. We both want to fuck him, and we want you to watch."
Anonymous woman, French Quarter, Mardi Gras, 2000

Living in the South fifty years,
I still don't know what it means.

The sense of place is brick.
Brick is the revelation,
and brick hides the secrets.
We built this, ourselves, alone, brick.
Brick splendid in the sun at Berkeley,
brick the tombs at Bruton Parish.
Brick the cellars at Scotchtown,
cool even in Virginia August.
Did Patrick Henry jail his wife,
or just keep her out of the sun?
Would I have done differently,
given time and place?

Exposed brick wall on Toulouse
between me and the screaming woman.
Fuck who?
Who watch?
Who knows?
Brick overhang above the porch,
protecting us from the thunderstorm at Monticello,
gathered with descendants of Jefferson
watching the incomprehensible rain.

Once at Monticello,
they asked us to leave Jefferson's crypt.
There was a snake –
A big snake.
Groundskeepers didn't want tourists frightened.
It wasn't a snake.
It was a dragon, my brother.

And I have chased the dragon fifty years.

Beginning of Lent, 2000

Bottom's Dream

"I'm pledged to the Queen of Heaven,
but all my life I've served the Elven Queen."

Nipple erect.
Tongue applied perfunctionally.
Precision required. No slobbering here.
A certain amount of technique.
We're not Walt Whitmanning here.
Pornographic? (Are we Walt Whitmanning here?)
No. Tongue in pursuit of....
Words, poems in pursuit of...

Ecstasy? Well, of course.
What wild pursuit!
Here now, always there.
Prefigured above from below.
The sought-after.
The point beyond ourselves.
The erect nipple, I mean.
Or God, the meaning of life, whatever.
The still point of the turning world.
Momentarily stilled.
While your back arches
enforcing the nipple at my lips
(a certain amount of technique required)
at the still point of the turning world.

Not what Sister Margaret Mary imagined for me,
I'm sure. Idle speculations of an idle mind.
But other organs are more focused
and more focusing,
as your hips move up and down,
rhythmically.
A certain amount of technique required,
to finish the dance.

For Oberon to find his Titania,
and Titania to find her Oberon,
and every man and woman
to know his and her own mate,
when all were lost and found,
and for all to be well.
For Bottom to know some hope
as the world joins the heavens,
prefigured above from below,
when asses heads find the Queen of Heaven
and serve the Elven Queen.

Feast of St. John the Baptist, 2000

Fifty Good Men in Sodom

Enter Lear with Cordelia in his arms: "Howl, howl, howl, howl!"

How'd it happen?
How did we lose control?
One moment I'm growing up in the '50s.
Suddenly, the screen fades, reforms,
and I'm in a new millennium.
A car passes me by:
"Ban partial birth abortions."

Ban them? Who'd ever allow them?
(I'm from the '50s, remember).
Basic test of civilization:
Will you protect your young?
No.

No. Shutting a door.
We shut different doors in the '50s.
One generation passes,
another comes,
and each has sufficient evil.

Between the '50s and the millennium
came the '60s and '70s.
I was there;
I am the man.
I know how we lost control.
As people always do, one step at a time.
I was only there for the sex and drugs,
I hope you understand.

And so Sodom had the evil of its day.
But it must have had fifty good men
(Keep bargaining, Abraham, keep bargaining).
The question is:
Did they feel vindicated
or ashamed,
when the first drops of fire fell?

Feast of Mary Magdalen, 2000

Walking the Walls

"A town I love so well."

The gentle land hurts us to poetry still.
Green, pleasant hills, ordered farms,
and terrible beauties abide.
Memories of hunger
imposed on us by others.
Imposed on others by ourselves.
Finally, self-imposed.
The final protest against all history,
the banshee wail of trash can lid on pavement,
announces the end of hunger
and the endless rebirth of hunger.

Two of us walk the walled city of Derry.
My friend points to the bog side,
"The Catholic plantation."
On the other side,
"The Protestant plantation."
If I lived here, we'd live in separate towns.
When my mother's people built
the plantations of Virginia,
the war was already here.
The Protestants of Derry starved for weeks.
The Catholics would hunger for centuries.

But we two play rugby
and so have no religion.
A violent sport unites us.
A religion of peace divides us.
The only remedy for mutual hunger,
the elements of our undoing.

Perhaps the IRA will decommission.
Perhaps the English Army will leave,
leave us to our hunger and distrust
that stalks school girls on the path
and festers in the farmland.

Bobby Sands twenty years in his grave.
He and the starving man haunt Derry still.
The hunger abides
in this green and pleasant land.

Feast of all Saints, 2001

Surfing Above Choo-Choo

for Becky, again

Red plastic toward the sight line;
always aim high.
Not red sails in the sunset.
Not that romantic.
Be still.
Keep the front of the boat right.

Right is an acute angle
toward the sight line.
Acute, neither direct nor obtuse.
And always high.
Lean back in the boat.
Relax.
Let the wave carry you in.

"The perfect way is without difficulty."
But don't let the koan distract you
or you'll go upside down.
Not the worst of fates,
but not what you want.

What you want is without difficulty.
The water will ferry you in
and point you right,
toward the sight line.
And all you see is
water and shore,
shore and trees,
with the sweep of the wave
under the boat,
like wind
under the wings of birds
who know neither Zen
nor poetry.

But only the sight line before them,
water and shore,
shore and trees,
forgetful of the water
swirling behind them
over the rapids at Choo-Choo
to the river beyond.

Spring, 2000

Sending Names to Abydos

for Trudy

I couldn't recognize
your final face
etched beyond pain,
resting in an open casket.
In the wilderness of Orange,
Disneyland of illusion.

As they closed the casket,
your friend Tom,
in quiet protest,
asked us to insist:
a casual photograph,
as you always looked,
atop the casket.

The minister droned on
about your spirit free from your body,
soaring wild and free, like a swan.
I prayed for you alive somewhere,
looking as you always did
in that body, but restored,
as in Tom's photograph,
as once we sat beside the Nile,
sending names to Abydos.

Lent, 2001

Once Upon a Time

"And I'll be willing..."

When I was young, I used to drive
backroads of western Virginia
under the full moon until dawn,
listening to the radio reports:
which mines were open, which closed.
Which shifts went to work, which stayed home.
Sometimes, in the corners of my eyes
I'd glimpse elves behind the trees.
Drugs and a vivid imagination.
Although, once quite clearly I saw
a troll sitting insolently
on the edge of the road.

The elves have retreated now.
I don't drive backroads any more,
and I don't do white crosses.
I fly in airplanes;
I drink martinis
and watch the evening news.
The world is a serious place.

One day I'd like to drive
the backroads again
to know the world alive and magical
and hope to see an elf or two
even if it means facing
the troll at the edge of the road.

Samadien/All Saints, 2002

The Fashion of the World

"I mean, I don't know any professional whores."
Anonymous girl, Grafton Street

Every girl on Grafton Street must show her navel.
Brittany's wings have touched old Ireland:
the navels, the black thongs, the omnipresent tattoo
over the crack of the ass.
Not the most flattering fashion for the full figured.
The view from Brewley's window changes in twenty years.
The Celtic tiger has pounced.
Ireland out-incomes England.
Living well is the only revenge.

The congregation at Saint Teresa thins
but remains, seemingly devout.
Praying for immigrants from within and without.
The Irish exiles: Liverpool, Australia, America.
Losing themselves.
How could they not, caught between worlds.
The Irish immigrants: Croats, Serbs, Bulgarians
begging in Dublin's alleyways.
Some things change, some remain.

O'Donoghue's is a snug place,
big enough for worlds to collide.
A traditional fiddler strikes a reel.
A woman with a shamrock tattoo claps and dances
badly out of time.
How could she not, caught between worlds.
German tourists with Sony cameras
struggle to catch the moment.
The fiddler fiddles on, thinking nothing.

Nothing but the music, as exiles dance.

Mass for the Immigrants,
2002 Shelbourne Hotel

Poets and Poetry

"Paddy Kavanaugh? Aye, I know people who knew him –
a drunk and a nuisance."

"A drunk and a nuisance."
The poet of *The Hunger* dismissed.
"Diss'd."
Poetry makes nothing happen.
Even in Ireland.
Pegasus, like Icarus,
flies too high.
Wings ignite, crash and burn.

Poetry makes nothing happen.
Words echo dead generations
or else they say nothing at all.
We bend our knees at St. Teresa's,
or we shut up and go home.

Our mission is to find what's lost
and been found and lost again.
Casting the find into today's idiom
to be found and lost again.

Nothing new, always new,
burnished in a moment of fashion.
Before the crash and burn,
the circus animal's desertion.

Poetry makes nothing happen
but steers the drunk and the nuisance
until he faces home at last.

Feast of St. Bridget of Sweden, 2003

Voices

"Up against the wall, motherfucker/Tear down the wall."

Language enslaves us.
So do the best you can.

The onslaught of Anglo-Saxon on Celtic;
The onslaught of Norman French on Anglo-Saxon.
Controlling Latin, twisting evolving English.
Castellano misrepresenting Quechua.
Before earth and Eternity,
Swords over words.

Do the best you can.

The schoolboy struggles to learn
the helping verbs
(Jesus, the helping verbs)
to the tune of "Jingle Bells:"

be, being, been, am, is, are, was, were, has, have, had…

The room spins, turns black,
the only sounding note: *being.*

The boy survives,
falls in love, once, twice, three times.

The stumbling words that told you what my heart felt.

Foolish things, scraps of song.
Words claim, fail, make amends:

deny, affirm, reconcile.

The boy becomes a monkey,
chattering in a tree.
The limb breaks;
The monkey falls into a river
and becomes a fish.

The fish swims silently, downriver.
The river widens, the land falls away
and becomes an ocean.

The fish becomes a dolphin
and hears a dolphin call his name.
He surfaces, breaks the light,
and hears other dolphins
calling one another
by name: *being.*

Language liberates us.
So, do the best you can.

Twenty-Fifth Sunday in Ordinary Time, 2002

World without End

for my grandmother
"Well, we're going to live 'til we die."

When does a world die?

When my grandmother grew up
men still remembered Chancellorsville.
Men who fought for Lee in the Wilderness,
men who marched all night with Jackson
and entered battle at full run.

I drive south
from Mosby's confederacy
through Fauquier
around the Wilderness
past Chancellorsville
to make funeral arrangements,
and I remember her memories.

History is not the trap.
Memory is the succubus
that seduces us
that beckons us
and forbids us
that rides us through the night
to connect us.

History drains the life,
forces it into black and white
onto pages in books
into issues of black and white
that protect us from life.

History teaches us
men fought for or against slavery.
For her grandfathers,
life was not so simple.

They fought their own fight,
lived their own lives,
died without regrets.

Worlds die when memories die,
when none can remember
those who remembered
the real life,
the life of action and toil.

Worlds die.
But the world remains.
The earth endureth forever,
a field of action
where we live 'til we die
begetting memory and loss
to connect us.

World without end.

Feast of St. Barnabas, 2003

Escaping Gracefully

for the Dixie Chicks
"Been a long time gone."

We're all a generation
or two or three removed
from the farm.
From Ireland.
Much the same thing:
the plow, the fiddle, the mandolin.
The connection
to the land.

We escaped gracefully
to good universities.
Phi Beta Kappa.
To good law schools.
Manhattan.
The suburbs.
The good life.

What did we lose?
The farm?
Ireland?
The connection
to the land?

All this
and more.
Our souls.
Remember those?

They hang in the balance.
Not in going back
to Ireland
to the farm
to the connection
to the land.

All good things,
but something more primal.
The connection
to ourselves
to one another.
Individually.
Collectively.
Together.
Our souls.
Remember those?

Our Lady of Perpetual Help, 2003

At the Hour of Our Death

for my mother

Without hope or reason
I rushed down the hospital corridor.
The doctors said hours
before you'd regain consciousness.
My heart told me minutes.
I didn't want you to be alone.

Our eyes met.
Your fingers searched your throat.
No incision.
You understood.
No incision.
No operation.
Inoperable.
No hope or reason.
"Nothing more we can do."

The last night, against odds,
you sat upright once again.
As a child might
supported by your mother.
Your sons beside you.
An ungainly pieta for a moment.
Then it was finished.

Heaven aches for its Queen
as a child cries for his mother.

Feast of the Immaculate Conception, 2003

Quickening the Pace

Like a horse returning to stable,
the pace quickens
as I turn toward home.
My mind wanders
to an indoor ring
a frigid February night.
A series of in and outs
without reins or stirrups.
Relaxed, balanced,
letting the horse do the work.
Younger then;
no fear of falling.

Running now, not riding
I remember falls.
Training in snow and ice
marathons ago.
At the Ashland 10k
the first crowded turn,
a runner fell,
others went down,
I sprinted to the outside,
lucky that time.
Not always.

Now it's three layers
against the cold.
The pound of pavement
through the ankles,
into the knees
recalls old falls.
Avoiding new ones
when I can,
quickening the pace
toward home.

Octave of Christian Unity, 2004

A Midsummer's Night Dream

for those whose faith is known alone to God

They never told us
you were Catholic.
No matter.
How would I
have not noticed?
The same preoccupations.
The same metaphors.
The same delight in nature.
The same delight in ceremony.
The same insistence on both.
Despite it all,
you were one of us.

Not that you
would have said so.
That choice,
a step to the block.
Campion dead.
Jonson in prison.
Heads did roll.
You kept yours.
Don't blame you.

The public choice:
Catholic or Protestant.
No wonder, your famous
ironic smile.
In exile
we discover
every forest is Arden
and every night, midsummer's.

The private choice,
if choice there is:
Catholic or the pagan

longing of the blood.
Ceremony or Nature.
Queen of Heaven
or the Elvin Queen.
The one impossible choice.

Ours was prefigured
in the stars;
in the slow turning
of the fickle seasons;
the slower turning
of the constellations.

Green leaf to brown.
Rising to falling.
Palm to palm.
Lips to lips.
Love to love.
Life to life.
Falling to rising.
Ceremony of Nature
risen to the stars.

A midsummer's night dream.
A faith known alone to God.

Birth of Mary, 2004

Perhaps I'll Build with Words

for my father

Nothing spectacular.
Just a perfect right angle of wood.
White against a blue wall,
a small piece of chair railing
maybe six inches by two,
tucked in a back corner of our house,
an odd corner, between closet and bath.

My father built the chair railing
and the ceiling molding
throughout the house.
Like he built the dresser,
a perfect Williamsburg reproduction.
Although it took him two years
in time stolen
from business trips,
church commitments,
family obligations,
and, of course, golf.

But why this single piece?
Why finish this corner?
This back corner,
where almost no one goes,
where almost no one sees.
Weren't all the other railings and moldings enough?
The business trips,
church commitments,
family obligations,
even the golf,
Weren't they enough?

No. Not for Dad.
Without this corner,
the rest would be meaningless.

This was his quiet statement,
a gratuitous act of perfection
finishing the job.

I almost contemplate
that right angle every day.
It's just below my elbow.
As I bend my arm
into a right angle,
pushing my body weight
into the door frame,
stretching my shoulder,
trying to get through
one more day without pain.

Dad's been gone thirty years.
Even he
couldn't have foreseen
my returning to the house
or my daily contemplation
of his work
(Could he?).
No.
His statement
was for himself.

I would never have finished the corner.
I don't have his skill
or his patience.
But I understand the sentiment.
The business trips,
church commitments,
family obligations.
Even the rugby
are not enough.

Perhaps one day
I'll build with words
my own right angle.
A small, quiet statement,

black letters against
a blank page
saying before eternity:
"I was here."

At least for a while.

Christmas, 2004

Through Earth, Eternity

"No ideas save in things."
The dead generations can teach us that.
But the saying is not truth itself,
only a path to truth.
And the way
in showing the way
forbids the way.

"More matter, less art."
A lifetime teaches us that.
A lifetime wrestling with words.
And finally, no art at all.

Only the slow ascent is left.
Up Humpback Rocks again.
Trail muddy with melting snow,
slipping underfoot,
caking on boots.
The new year's sun
Gleaming through bare trees.
The trail rising to the rocks,
to the view of endless valley.
Rocks, trees, mountains, light:
the face of eternity.

"Suffer me not to be separated."

Lent, 2004

The Paradox

for Frank and Julian

Between the orthodox
and the heresy of the heterodox
balances the paradox,
"Sin is behovely."
The dragon at the door,
curling around the orb of the world,
lying in wait
for a woman clothed with the sun.

When I was a boy of five,
my great-uncle would take me to church,
puffing a cigar right up to the church porch.
He'd put down the cigar,
we'd listen to the sermon
and go out again.
He'd retrieve the cigar,
light it,
and we'd walk home.

At the beach, he'd cast his line
into the surf in the late evening.
"Frank," I'd say, "you can't catch fish now."
He'd laugh, reel it in and show me:
It wasn't even baited.
He'd cast again
and puff the cigar.

That night, a bonfire
and party on the beach
would wake me.
He'd tell me to go back to sleep.
"They're pirates.
When you grow up,
you'll be a pirate, too."

One day, he slumped over at work.
My parents left us with my grandmother
and rushed to the hospital.
He died on the operating table.

A cigar is just a cigar.
It's not a Freudian symbol.
A cigar, not even a sin,
an inconsequential mortal vice.
And I'm not quite a pirate.

Your mind is locked from me now,
as it was when I was five.
What went through your mind
while you puffed the cigar,
reeled in the line,
slumped at your desk?

The paradox:
sin is behovely.
We must lose ourselves
to find ourselves.
True enough:
we lose ourselves
in a puff of smoke,
the escapades on the beach,
the piracy of our thoughts,
the final tumors in the brain.

But in losing ourselves,
do we find ourselves at last?
If we do, is it in spite of
or because of
the puff of smoke,
the escapades on the beach,
the piracy of our thoughts
and deeds,
And what we have failed to do?

Lent, 2005

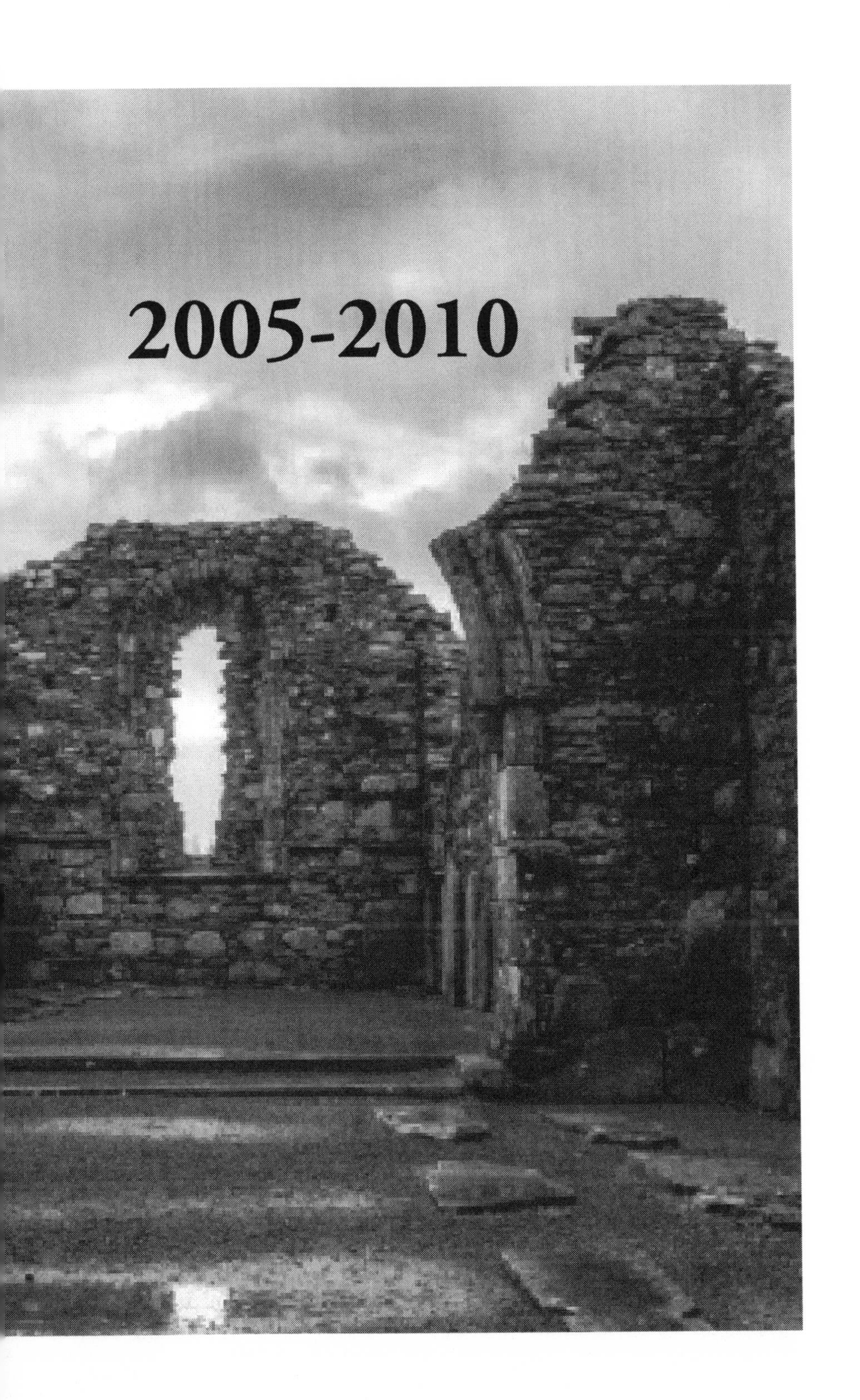
2005-2010

The Delay of Eagles

"The eagles are coming!
The eagles are coming!"
Tolkien's fantasy.
The cavalry to the rescue.
The eleventh hour reprieve.
The "eucatastrophe."
The happy ending.
It makes a good story.

History's not like that.
No eagles came for Constantine.
He died before the walls
of the City of God,
baited like a bear,
against all odds,
abandoned by the West.

There's glory in that.
Constantine chose his end.
He died with his men,
stripping himself of insignia
to be with them
at the end of all things.

Martyrdom becomes temptation.
The eagles delay.
They will not come for us.

So we live
not unlike Constantine,
choosing what we must,
one slow day
after another.

Advent, 2005

The Tides at Gloucester

The tide inches up
the dock's ladder.
The kayaks wait patiently,
the kayakers less so.

To live with the tides
now requires a conscious decision.
We are used to the time of Richmond,
ninety minutes away.
There, time is measured exactly
by digital clocks that change
automatically with the seasons.
And we make decisions on what we think we know.

Here, the motion of the tides
is less exact.
Wind and rain work subtle changes
in depth and flow.
The tides allow the moments out of time,
when the deer hunter's stand is empty
and the mind floats free through the marsh.

But the tides are more demanding
than the clocks of Richmond.
They sweep us toward the full tide,
where we approach what we know we do not know.

Not ashes to ashes
but ashes to water.

Feast of Saint John Laterean, 2007

Maddie in the Rain

"Dic nobis, Maria. Quid vidisti in viam?"

The first day the nest was abandoned
there were still four eggs intact.
The second day there was one.
The third day there were none.

We had watched you mate,
build the nest
and guard your eggs,
turning with the sun each day.

What drove you away?

I had called you Maddie,
maybe not the best choice.

We saw you flying away
the next day.
Then you were gone.

Or so it seemed.

But there you were
outside my window
on the twisted wire.

Staring into the rain
of a hundred-year Northeaster
flooding on the east coast.

There had been snow
for Easter.

And soon thirty-three dead
in the Blue Ridge.

Maddie,
what do you see
in the rain?

Easter, 2007

Maddie Redux

She's returned.

Twice now.
Each time
in spring.

Same dove.
Same tree.
Same branch.

New nests.
New babies.
Familiar problems:

children who
won't leave
the nest.

But the eventual,

final flights:
first theirs.
Then hers.

Leaving us
to await
the return.

Beginning of Ordinary Time, 2008

Memory of Eagles

Alone on the water
distractions disappear
behind the kayak.
Past the osprey nest
abandoned for winter
beyond the empty boat house
into the quiet inlet.
Out of the wind and current,
the rain mere drizzle.
Past the point where
the eagle soared over our heads
and settled into the tree.
Memories recede,
but they persist,
and they suffice.

Third Sunday in Ordinary Time, 2008

Vicksburg's Falling

"Duty is the noblest word in the English language."
Robert E. Lee

Fourth of July sun
glistens on Wilson Creek.
Paddles toward the Ware
enter water effortlessly
producing contentment.

But in the morning
the red, white and blue
bunting at the courthouse
is damp with rain.

Out on 17,
you see the vultures first
on the side of the road,
vertical over the fallen doe.

Vicksburg's falling,
towers are burning,
Spartan bones
glisten in the sun.
Loyal to our country.
Semper fi.

Vietnam.
Afghanistan.
Iraq.
How many more?

We are not immune:
nature red
in tooth and claw.

July 5, 2008

Mirror to Nature

Tucked
into the narrow channel
by Wilson Farms
the boat bobs
in shallow water.
The kingfisher flashes.
The eagles circle
in the gyre.
The earth endures
while we wander.

End of Ordinary Time, 2008

Winter Full

Gaude

Winter full
moon over
Wilson Creek.
The solstice
steals upon us
silently
under the fullness
of light.

Advent, 2008

Triduum

Easter Sequence

Holy Thursday

The floating dock
is finished;
completed in time
for the season.

The pilings trimmed
to preserve
the sight line
to where
the oncoming tide
swirls past a point of land.

A floating dock.
Easier to get
in and out
of the kayaks
as we age.

A hedge
against the future.

Good Friday

Osprey flying
in the morning light,
underneath, a fish
clutched in her talon.

The ospreys are back
in numbers, before
the herons, before
the egrets,
filling every nest.

Back to the Bay;
back to Wilson Creek;
back from low numbers.

Continuing
an existence
as precarious
as our own.

Saturday: in Between

(Dragon Run is a river and cypress swamp on the edge of Gloucester County)

Dragon Run,
past Eve and Adam,
descending
into something primal:
the water dark.
The cypress no longer forested.
The hunter's deer stand empty.
The night heron
too far north.
We paddle single file
through narrow water.
The dark sky gathers
confusing water, earth, sky.
Wind and rain
overtake us.
Almost at world's end
the river widens
and we take out
under a canopy
of spring trees.

Easter

An everyday
Sunday.
Sky bright
but cool.
Too much wind
for open water.
So we put in
from the new dock
for the safety
of the marsh.

The bay will wait
for another day.

Easter, 2009

Palace of Wisdom

The egrets wait for us
at the mouth of the channel
near Wilson Farms.
One of them leads us.
Still, until
we paddle close.
Then she glides
to the next
overhanging branch
and again and again
as we approach,
down the channel
to the marsh beyond.
And we follow
as best we can
in the full
simplicity
of life.

Feast of the Immaculate Conception, 2009

Home

I was born
to love the sea;
the sound of breakers
lulling me to sleep.
At dawn, the surf,
the sun, the wind
like the play of words
in my mind.

But we are drawn
from what we love
into the cities,
the give and take
of commerce,
endless compromises
leading nowhere.

We make the way
back to what matters.
Not to the sea directly,
but through other waters.
From the rivers of our diaspora
we are called.
The desire to return
to the sea, our home.

Feast of the Ascension, 2012

Easter

Wisteria
has taken over the lane.
A season of no winter
gives over to spring.
No snow.
No rain.

Dragon Run
is choked
with undergrowth.
Water low,
passage impossible
without rain.

Every season
is impossible;
an adventure,
a pilgrimage
of grace.

Easter, 2012

After Our Exile

Nothing out of the ordinary.

Calm, clear day.
An easy paddle
through the channel
past Wilson Farms.

Beyond the boathouse
the solitary egret
waits in silent anticipation.

It tucks into its awkward,
impossible flight
leading us into the marsh,
past the fallen tree,
toward the bridge.

The tide changes.
We turn toward home.
The sun at our backs
glistens on the water.

Everything out of the ordinary.

Solemnity of Mary, 2015

Saint Thomas Synagogue

American Virgin Islands

"Put sand on the floor.
Keep your voices down,
don't let them find us."
Back, through centuries.
Exodus to home.

I don't share the faith,
but I know the feeling.
They come through the heat,
up from cruise ships, from Brooklyn.
Pilgrims up the steep hill
to an impossible place
with an impossible name.
To remember,
to re-enact,
to find a way.

As we all do.
Searching through the centuries,
through Ireland, Rome, Palestine.
Sand on the floor.
Silent voices
bent in prayer.

To the place with the impossible name.
Saint Thomas Synagogue.
"A perfect place,"
the guide says,
offering prayer shawls.

"Put sand on the floor,
don't let them find us."
Searching, alone,
different together,
on the way home.

Epiphany, 2016

Dominican Republic

Here there is no time.
No clocks in the kitchens.
No clocks in the bedrooms.
No shelves where
the flotsam and jetsam
of everyday life
can hide.

Here there is only sun,
and sand, and open sea.
Nothing between us
and the weather.
Nothing between us
and time.

November, 2015

2012 - 2022

Dolphins

"What is that?"
"Que es eso?"
The primal question.
Dave's index
finger points.
The interrogative.
The indicative.
The need to know.

They've come
up the Chesapeake.
The Bay.
The Bay of the Mother
of God.
The Spanish named it.

The Dolphins
in Wilson Creek.
A pod – six?
Swimming quickly
past the kayaks.
Chasing prey.
Finishing quickly.
Returning slowly.
Time to play.

Brushing against
the kayaks.
Returning slowly
to the bay.
The Bay.
The Mother
of all things.

Lent, 2019

Thin Places

An everyday paddle
past the bend in the creek
into Wilson Farms.
The blade of the paddle
turning the water.
The sun turning the light
on the blade turning water.
The kingfisher chatters overhead.
An everyday paddle.
And yet.
Our ancestors talked
of thin places
Where worlds intersect:
Glastonbury becomes Avalon.
Wilson Creek becomes an image
of a new, better world to come.

Lent, 2019

Redemption Songs

for Bob Marley

Stay to the left.
Shift with the left.
Mind the hedges
on your left.
You can do this.
Then, a familiar name
on the road sign.
Athenry.
You know the town:
Lo li, the fields of Athenry.
But you don't
know the town.
Never been there.
Only a song
sung on a rainy rugby pitch.
Like the songs of heaven.
Redemption songs.
All I ever had,
Redemption Songs.

Ordinary Time, 2019

Day of the Dead

for all the dead

November.
The dead cling to us
or we to them.
They speak to us
in dreams of Halloween,
in tiresome days
of failing light.
In the fog over the creek
they speak to us.

But we cannot answer,
constrained by time and place,
cannot articulate the loss,
the mourning unachieved.
We cannot answer.

So we wait.

Feast of Saint John Lateran, 2021

Invasions of the Imagination

Imagination invades memory,
twisting recollections
into something more meaningful
and more pleasant.
The Pre-Raphaelites re-invented Camelot.
The Oxford Movement created the High Church.
My UDC great aunts birthed the Lost Cause.

Me, I'm not immune.
I've taken childhood memories
and turned them to idylls of innocence.
But it didn't really live that way.

So we stand accused.
The corrective is as clear as Scholasticism.
"The heart is desperately wicked
and deceitful above all else."
True, but not so pleasant.

So we stand corrected.
History, at best, is historical fiction.
We stand corrected.

But where do we go
from here?

Feast of Saint Cloud, an honest man, 2021

Acknowledgments

I like to read historical fiction. So, at the end of a novel set in turn-of-the century New York, I'm likely to see acknowledgments from the author for the people who, say, helped him understand the public transit system at the beginning of the 20th Century, which is all well and proper. Since virtually all of my poetry flows directly from life experiences, I don't have any acknowledgments like that.

But since it is a book of poetry, there are lots of other people I should acknowledge: Shakespeare and Bob Dylan; Yeats and Little Feat; Paddy Kavanagh and the Dixie Chicks. And so many more. Even though I try to keep my poems conversational, the allusions keep slipping in, sometimes directly, sometimes in slightly different forms.

For example, the title of the poem "Gentle Rain of Heaven" is an allusion to Shakespeare, but I doubt many people would notice that, because I try to draw attention to the epigram, "Now Shakespeare, he's in the alley" ... which is pure Dylan and pure fun. But then Shakespeare and Dylan disappear from the poem, until the last lines which are not so much an allusion to Portia's speech near the end of *The Merchant of Venice* as an echo: "The quality of mercy is not strained / it droppeth as the gentle rain of heaven / upon the place below."

There are a lot of allusions, near allusions, and echoes throughout the poems, and I gratefully acknowledge the poets who have gone before me and left such a treasure chest for me to steal from.

On a more practical note, I want to thank my publisher, Jeanne Johansen, for taking a chance on this book, my editor, Cindy Freeman, and all the High Tide Publications group who have been so supportive of me, especially my friend Sharon Canfield Dorsey who put the deal together and cheered me on.

Thanks for reading *Chasing the Dragon*. Reviews are very important to authors. If you enjoyed this book, please leave an honest review on your favorite site.

Thanks!

About the Author

I was born and raised in Richmond, Virginia. I went to UVA, and having no idea what I was going to do with my life, I hung around and got an MA, an M. Ed., and even finished the course work for a PhD. But I never finished my dissertation (actually, I never started one: my attention span isn't that long).

Still not knowing what I wanted to do with my life, I took a job at Virginia Commonwealth University, where I taught for twenty years, both full time and in the night school.

I also started a rugby career of playing and coaching for over twenty-five years. I wasn't much good, but I loved the game.

From academia, I drifted into market research, which proved a good fit. For twenty-five years, Rebecca Day and I ran Kinzey & Day Qualitative Research. We had a good run, working for clients such as Hilton, McDonald's, Anthem, and various hospitals and universities.

The poems in this collection were written over those twenty-five years, in moments stolen from teaching, work, rugby and parish commitments – moments in and out of time.

Made in the USA
Middletown, DE
15 April 2022